Crowdfunding on Steroids

GENERAL SOLICITATION UNDER NEW RULE 506

Author: Douglas Slain, J.D., M.A.

Table of Contents

CHAPTER ONE: New Rules

The new Rule 506 changes everything.

The SEC has lifted an 80-year ban on general solicitation and start-ups and other Issuers for the first time can use public advertising to sell private offerings. Startups are now able to use advertising and general solicitations to fund private placements!

The new Rule 506 may prove to be the answer to the prayers of startups frustrated with existing fund sourcing platforms. *But it also has hidden dangers that will cause many issuers to continue to use the "old Rule 506."*

Among the new Rule 506 strengths, observe:

- The amount that can be raised is unlimited

- There is no requirement for review of the offering under any Blue Sky laws (state securities regulations)

- There is no review of the offering by the SEC

- Solicitations can be online or offline

- Solicitations can be made to anyone!

Sales (as opposed to solicitations) must be to accredited investors, and issuers must be able to verify that any actual investor is "accredited." Also, proposed rules will require issuers to send the SEC all marketing copy; as of this writing, however, there is no need to send copies of solicitation materials to the SEC (or to state regulators).

Soon you will start to see the following:

- Emails asking if you might be interested in learning about investing in someone's project

- Videos of founders and entrepreneurs soliciting your interest in their projects

- Links on websites inviting you to click through to learn more about an investment

- Mobile apps with increasingly creative solicitation

Private placement memorandum and related offering documents continue to be mandatory.

Investment funds now will have access to a much wider pool of potential investors than before, subject to separate rules and regulations promulgated by their own, separate regulators.

CHAPTER TWO: Rule 506
Questions and Answers

Q: How have private offerings been sold historically?

Rule 506 of Regulations D establishes a "safe harbor" under Section 4(a) (2) of the Securities Act of 1933 for sales of securities not involving a public offering. Compliance with Rule 506 means an issuer does not need to register with the SEC or any state neither securities regulator, nor does it need to file reports with the SEC, other than a Form D within 15 days of the first sale of any offering. Under the existing Rule 506 exemption, *which some issuers will opt to continue to use,* an issuer may sell an unlimited number of securities under the following conditions:

- the issuer may not use general solicitation or general advertising;

- the issuer may sell to an unlimited number of accredited investors, but only up to 35 other investors who are "sophisticated";

- if non-accredited investors are included in the offering, additional disclosures are made to them; and

- the securities issued are "restricted."

Q: How will most private offerings be sold in the future?

The new Rule 506 adds a new subsection (c) that says that an issuer may use general solicitation or general advertising when offering and selling securities as long as:

- all purchasers turn out to be accredited investors (or the issuer reasonably believed they are accredited at the time of sale);

- the issuer takes reasonable steps to verify the accredited investor status of each purchaser; and

- the issuer complies with other applicable provisions of Regulation D.

Q: How has verification occurred until now?

Issuers have relied on the investor's representation that he or she is an "accredited investor" under one of the categories in rule 501(a).

Q: How will verification occur now?

Under the new rules, issuers must take "reasonable steps to verify the accredited investor status." New Rule 506(c) (2) (ii) includes several non-exclusive methods to satisfy the verification requirement such as:

- reviewing any IRS form that reports the purchaser's income for the two most recent years and obtaining a signed statement from the purchaser that he or she has a reasonable expectation of reaching the income level necessary to qualify as an accredited investor during the current year, or

- reviewing bank, brokerage or other statements, and a consumer report from at least one of the nationwide consumer reporting agencies dated within three months, and obtaining a written representation from the purchaser that all liabilities necessary to make a determination of net worth have been disclosed, or

- obtaining written confirmation from a registered broker-dealer, SEC-registered investment adviser, licensed attorney or certified public accountant that the issuer has taken reasonable steps to verify the purchaser's accredited investor status.

Note that there is a "grandfather" provision in new Rule 506(c) (2) (ii) (D). For existing investors who were accredited investors in a Rule 506(b) offering prior to the effective date of Rule 506(c), a self-certification of accreditation status at the time of sale in a new offering by the same issuer under Rule 506(c) will satisfy the verification requirement in Rule 506(c).

Q: What is general solicitation?

General solicitation or general advertising includes using websites accessible to the general public, using a widely disseminated email or social media campaign, or using print media, such as a newspaper or magazine ad. Issuers are *not required to use general solicitation* and may continue to engage in private placements as they did under "old Rule 506" under new Rule 506(b). Form D is being revised to add a box that must be checked by those issuers who use general solicitation or general advertising in the offering.

Q: Who is an accredited investor?

An accredited investor is someone who is not in need of enhanced protection by the SEC. The new amendments did not change the definition of "accredited investor" in Rule 501(a). An accredited investor remains:

- an individual with a net worth greater than $1 million (exclusive of the value of a primary residence), either individually or jointly with the individual's spouse

- a natural person with income exceeding $200,000 in each of the two most recent years or joint income with a spouse whose annual income exceeds $300,000 for those years and a reasonable expectation of the same income level in the current year

- a trust with assets in excess of $5 million, not formed to acquire the securities offered, whose purchases are directed by a "sophisticated person" as described in Rule 506(b)(2)(ii)

- a charitable organization, corporation or partnership with assets exceeding $5 million

- a bank, insurance company, registered investment company, business development company or small business investment company

- an employee benefit plan, within the meaning of the Employee Retirement Income Security Act, if a bank, insurance company or registered investment adviser makes the investment decisions, or if the plan has total assets in excess of $5 million

- a director, executive officer or general partner of the issuer or

- an entity in which all the equity owners are accredited investors.[9]

Q: Is the SEC going to change the definition of accredited investor?

The SEC has solicited comments with respect to the current definition as mandated by the Dodd-Frank Act to review the current standard and has posed a number of questions asking for comment.

Q: Who is a bad actor?

The Dodd-Frank Act required the SEC to adopt rules to prohibit use of Rule 506 for offerings in which certain "bad actors" are involved, whether or not general solicitation is used. The SEC has adopted rules disallowing an issuer from selling securities in reliance on Rule 506 if the issuer, its board members, certain of its officers and its large shareholders, among others, have experienced a "disqualifying event." This is similar to existing bad actor rules, such as those found in Rule 505 of Regulation D, which relies on the disqualification provisions set forth in Rule 262 of Regulation A.

Q: What is a covered person?

Any issuer wanting to make use of the exemption provided by Rule 506 (whether or not the issuer engages in general solicitation or general advertising) will need to exercise reasonable care to prevent a covered person with a disqualifying event from participating in the offering "covered persons" include:

- the issuer of the securities, including its affiliates and predecessors, and directors, certain officers, general partners and managing members

- individual holders of 20 percent or more of the voting control of the issuer

- investment managers (and their principals) of pooled investment funds and

- promoters and those compensated for soliciting investors (including the principals of entities performing such services)

Officers of an issuer will be "covered persons" if they participate in the offering. Participation in an offering could include such activities such as due diligence activities, preparation of disclosure documents, and communications with prospective investors or other offering participants.

Q: What will disqualify a covered person?

"Disqualifying events" include:

- convictions for securities-related crimes that have occurred within 10 years of the proposed sale of securities (5 years for covered person who are the issuer and its predecessors/affiliates)

- securities-related injunctions and restraining orders and similar sanctions such as SEC stop orders and US Postal Service false representation orders within 5 years prior to the proposed sale

- final orders from various banking agencies and regulators of securities, insurance and financial institutions that prohibit the covered person from engaging in the business of securities, insurance or banking or that are based upon fraudulent, manipulative or deceptive conduct and which were issued within 10 years of the proposed offering

- SEC disciplinary or cease-and-desist orders and

- suspension or expulsion from membership in a self-regulatory organization such as FINRA

Q: How about events before the new rules became effective?

Only events that occur *after* the new rules become effective will be considered "disqualifying events." However, issuers will need to disclose prior events if they would have been considered disqualifying under the new rules.

Q: What do I have to do if I want to be an issuer?

You need to identify and evaluate entities and individuals deemed covered persons such as directors, officers, promoters or prospective purchasers and determine whether any disqualifying events have occurred with respect to them. For events that occurred prior to the effective date of the rules, issuers will need to disclose information about such disqualifying events in their offering materials. After the effective date of the rules, if covered persons experience disqualifying events the issuer will no longer be able to rely upon the exemption from registration contained in Rule 506.

Q: What else should I know?

See the SEC's Fact Sheet regarding the lifting of the ban on general solicitation and advertising. Also, note that several other regulatory regimes still apply to general solicitation or general advertising and require compliance with Regulation D and other applicable laws. Not only must issuers still comply with applicable state securities laws but also with the Federal regulation of broker-dealers who participate in their offerings. Interestingly, the SEC has said it will closely monitor general solicitation and advertising activities. Chairman Mary Jo White has_said, "As we fulfill our mission to facilitate capital formation and maintain fair and efficient markets, the Commission must always focus on strong investor protections. We want this new market and the private markets in general to thrive in a safe and efficient manner, and these rules we adopt and propose are designed to facilitate that objective."

Q: Can you compare new and old Rule 506?

Under the new rules, issuers will be granted unprecedented access to legions of investors. Still, there are at least three reasons not to use the new rules, and issuers can elect to operate under the old rules if they choose.

1) Issuers who choose to offer securities in the new manner, and the persons associated with them, will need to comply with accredited investor

verification requirements and with the updated verification requirements as long as the offering are ongoing.

2) Issuers or affiliates may well be subject to the Exchange Act, and state requirements, as broker-dealers, if they or their sponsors do more than one offering per year. (Note that many believe that the transactional role of broker-dealers will change as a result of the lifting of the ban on general solicitation and general advertising).

3) *Proposed* rules may make public solicitations impracticable for many. See below.

Q: What is the impact of the Securities Exchange Act of 1934?

Lifting the ban on general solicitation may not open the flood gates for private placements as much as anticipated simply because of the exiting definition of a broker-dealer. If the officers, directors or employees of an issuer engage in the marketing and sale of securities to the public, including statements (whether oral or written) made by such affiliates of the issuer, they are broker-dealers under the Securities Exchange Act of 1934, unless exempted.

Section 3(a) (4)_of the Exchange Act defines a "broker" as any person engaged in the business of effecting transactions in securities for the account of others. Rule 3a4-1 contains "safe harbor" from this definition for the officers, directors and employees of an issuer, allowing them not to register if not compensated based on the sale of the securities, not currently registered as a broker-dealer, and not guilty of certain bad acts.

Also, if the security is sold through a registered broker-dealer, any "associated person" (a) must primarily perform tasks other than the sale of securities for the issuer, (b) cannot be and has not for the prior 12 months been, a registered broker-dealer, and (c) does not participate in more than one offering every 12 months. Also the associated person can only participate in written communications through the mail or email or text in response to inquiries from potential investors (no talking) and she or he can only perform administrative work with respect to the transaction.

Q: How will this affect VCs and other private funds?
Private funds, such as hedge funds, private equity funds and venture capital funds, are now be able to advertise without violating the Rule 506 exemption. Before doing so, however, they need to consider that private funds must comply with applicable requirements of the Investment Company Act of 1940 and the Investment Advisers Act of 1940, as well as the

Commodity Exchange Act and regulations of the Commodity Futures Trading Commission.

Q: What amendments has the SEC proposed but not implemented?

The SEC has proposed additional rules that will add significant requirements to Rule 506 offerings using general solicitation. These proposed rules will reduce the attractiveness of general solicitation offerings. See SEC's Fact Sheet regarding the proposed rules. Note that some of the proposed changes apply to Rule 506(c) offerings—those using general solicitation or general advertising—while some apply to **all** Rule 506 offerings.

Q: What are some of the proposed rules?

Issuers selling securities under Rule 506 will be required to file a Form D no later than 15 days following the first sale of securities. Issuers will, in addition, be required to file a Form D at least 15 days *prior* to engaging in general solicitation. Further, a "closing" Form D amendment will be required within 30 days of the termination of the offering. Issuers also will be required to provide additional information, such as:

- more information about the issuer, including information regarding its revenues and net asset value (which may be marked "Not Available to Public" if the issuer has not made the information public in general solicitation materials)

- under a broader definition of related persons and, for Rule 506(c) offerings, disclosure of each person who directly or indirectly controls the issuer, which will require beneficial owners with a significant equity stake to be disclosed

- the exact numbers of accredited and non-accredited investors participating in the offering, the amounts raised from each category and whether they are natural persons or legal entities

- the use of proceeds from offerings by issuers (other than pooled investment funds), including proposed payments to related persons

- whether offering proceeds will be used to repurchase or retire the issuer's existing securities, acquire assets, finance acquisitions of other businesses, or use as working capital or to discharge indebtedness

- whether any of the issuer's securities are traded on a national securities exchange, alternative trading system or other organized trading venue and, if applicable, the trading symbol and security identifier

- the issuer's website address, if any

- in Rule 506(c) offerings, the types of general solicitation used or planned to be used (such as mass mailings, email, public websites, social media, print media and broadcast media) and the methods used to verify accredited investor status.

Q: How about legends?

The SEC has proposed requirements that written general solicitation materials contain certain legends disclosing that: a) the securities may be sold only to accredited investors, b) are being sold pursuant to an exemption to the Securities Act, c) have not been reviewed by the SEC, and d) are subject to restrictions on transfer.

Private funds will be required to include a prominent disclosure that the securities are not subject to the protections of the Investment Company Act.

If the issuer is a private fund and includes information about past performance in its general solicitation materials, the issuer must provide information regarding the limitations of such information as an indicator of future performance.

Q: Is there a "proposed temporary" rule?

Yes; this rule will require issuers using general solicitation or general advertising (i.e., a Rule 506(c) offering) to submit "any written communication that constitutes a general solicitation" to the SEC through a new online intake page *before* such materials is used. The SEC has said that these materials will not be made available to the public but has not stated that they will be treated as confidential and it is not clear whether they could be available pursuant to a Freedom of Information Act request.

Q: What if an issuer did not comply in the past?

Under the proposed changes, an issuer will be disqualified from relying on Rule 506 if it or its predecessors or affiliates failed to comply with the Form D filing requirements within the past five years. A one-year disqualification period would commence upon the filing of all required notices on Form D or amendments thereto. Such disqualification would not apply to the offering for which the issuer failed to file a Form D or an amendment thereto, but would apply to any offerings commenced thereafter. Issuers will be provided a 30-day cure period to address the issuer's first failure to file a timely Form D or Form D amendment in connection with a particular offering. Issuers will otherwise be permitted to obtain a waiver upon a showing of good cause.

Q: I have been conducting a private placement prior to the effective date of Rule 506c—September 23, 2013—and I have sold to a few non-accredited investors in full compliance with Rule 506b. After

September 23, I want to convert my offering to a 506c and start general solicitation, of course selling only to verified accredited investors. But will I have lost my exemption since a 506c offering cannot include non-accredited investors?

As of this writing, the SEC has not commented on this fact pattern. It has confirmed that any general solicitation occurring after September 23 will not affect the exempt status of a former 506b offering otherwise in compliance. But the SEC has not advised on whether converting the 506b to a 506c will create problems under the SEC integration doctrine or otherwise if non-accredited investors are integrated into the new 506c offering.

CHAPTER THREE: Funding

When doing an equity or debt raise for an early stage business, you need to:

- Reduce to writing an executive summary, business plan, and financial projections

- Determine the structure for the proposed offering

- Incorporate or form a limited liability company

- Prepare a private placement memorandum, investor questionnaire and subscription agreement

- File exemption documents with regulators

- Identify and present to accredited investors

- Prepare term sheet(s)

- Execute appropriate investor document

Once you have prepared an executive summary, a business plan and financial projections, you need offering documents, as follows:

I. A **Private Placement Memorandum** is a document that discloses all relevant and material information that a reasonable investor would want to know before deciding whether or not to engage in a proposed transaction.

A PPM is different from a prospectus. The term "prospectus" is used when referring to an offering document for registered securities whereas the term "private placement memorandum" is used in reference to securities that are exempt from registration under Regulation D.

Checklist of what *can* be in a PPM:

- Suitability Standards for Investors
- Summary of the Securities Offering
- Risk Factors
- Capitalization of the Company
- Use of Proceeds from the Securities Offering
- Dilution
- Plan of Distribution of the Securities
- Selected Financial Data
- Analysis of Financial Condition and Results of Operation
- The Business of the Company
- Management and Compensation
- Certain Transactions (transactions between the Company and its shareholders, officers, directors or affiliates)
- Principal Shareholders

- Terms of the Securities Offered

- Description of Capital Stock of the Company

- Tax Matters

- Legal Matters

- Experts

- Documents Available for Inspection

- Financial Statements

- Projections

- Exhibits

II. An **Investor Questionnaire** is crucial for private placement offerings. Each type of offering has its own requirements for investors. A company must have a reasonable belief that its potential investors meet those requirements. That determination must be made before the potential investor can be given offering documents (PPM, business plan, term sheet, etc.) or specifics regarding the offering. This is done by having potential investors complete an investor questionnaire. The SEC has made it clear that a minimal "check the box" approach is not sufficient. In other words, you cannot have an investor questionnaire that merely asks "Are you an accredited investor?" and then "yes" and "no" check boxes. What the SEC wants is a questionnaire that requests specific information concerning such things such as the respondent's investment experience, investment goals, age, employment history, education, income and net worth.

III. The **Subscription Agreement** is the "investment contract" for purchasing the securities. Typically an investor will complete this document, with a signed Investment Questionnaire, before writing a check.

IV. The **Term Shee**t will not be needed until you have found a seriously interested investor. A term sheet is a non-binding agreement setting forth the key terms and conditions of the proposed transaction. A term sheet serves as a template for a more developed and detailed legal document. Once the parties agree on the details laid out in the term sheet, a binding contract that conforms to the term sheet details is drafted. A term sheet lies the groundwork for ensuring that the parties involved in a business transaction is in agreement on most major aspects of the deal, thereby precluding the possibility of a misunderstanding. It also ensures that expensive legal charges involved in drawing up a binding agreement or contract is not incurred prematurely. Terms sheets cover the more important aspects of a deal, without going into every minor detail and contingency covered by a binding contract. For example, a term sheet from a venture capital company that is investing in an early-stage company may contain such details as the amount of investment, the percentage stake sought, anti-dilutive provisions and valuation.

CHAPTER FOUR: Private Placements

A private placement occurs when an individual or company secures funding from an investor, whether equity or debt. A private placement memorandum (PPM) is a disclosure document that outlines the terms and conditions of that offering. The document is similar to a business plan except the emphasis is on disclosure of facts rather than projected results. If you are trying to raise capital by offering a promissory note or a piece of the equity to private investors you need a private placement memorandum that allows the advantages of SEC Regulation D exemption rules 504, 505, or (most likely) 506.

The PPM must contain all relevant information about your company and its business as well as any other information that might possibly be considered material by a potential investor.

The PPM should be accompanied by a subscription agreement and an investor questionnaire. The subscription
agreement is a contract to purchase a specified number of securities at an agreed price. It must contain a

statement that the investor has received and reviewed the PPM and that she/he is aware of the risk factors and is a suitable investor. The investor questionnaire solicits information about the investor's background, employment and investment experience. It is used to confirm the investor's investment sophistication.

There are two common types of securities that companies offer via a regulation D: equity and debt.

Equity Offering

Equity securities consist of shares for a corporation or membership units for an LLC. They represent a portion of the ownership interest in the company. Stockholders are entitled to vote on company matters and must receive all key information about the company, including financial statements, on a regular basis.

Debt Offering

Debt securities usually consist of notes representing debt obligations of the company, with a specified interest rate, maturity date and repayment amount. A company should only offer debt securities if it can demonstrate that it has the ability to repay the debt.

CHAPTER FIVE: Regulation D

Regulation D is a United States Federal program created under the Securities Act of 1933, as amended in 1982, that allows companies the ability to raise capital through the sale of equity or debt securities without registration.

There are 3 Regulatory "Rules" which are relied upon to raise capital. These rules allow for different amounts of capital, different types of investors and different methods for conducting an offering:

- 504(up to $1 million)
- 505(up to $5 million)
- 506(any amount)

The Reg D programs were designed to provide an exemption to sell securities in a private capital raise without registering the securities and also to identify the appropriate documentation for properly accepting and using the capital.

There are 2 basic types of Regulation D Offerings.

- An equity offering occurs when a company sells partial ownership in a company, usually using corporate stock or LLC membership units. Equity offerings are preferred by most early stage companies because there are no debt payments; instead, the investors receive a return when the company profits and those profits are shared.A debt offering occurs when a company sells one or more promissory notes to investors. A debt offering is similar to a business loan; instead of a bank providing the financing, investors lend funds to the firm.

A Regulation D Offering involves several preliminary steps:

1) Determine structure

The first step in an offering is properly setting the structure. Structuring includes determining how much of the company to sell (in equity transactions), setting the maturity date and rate of return for the promissory notes (in debt situations), electing which Reg D program to use, and establishing minimum and maximum offering amounts.

2) Prepare offering documents

Regulation D offering documents commonly include:

- The Private Placement Memorandum (PPM) is the document that discloses all required information to the investors about the company, proposed operations, the transaction structure and the terms of the investment offered.

- The Investor Questionnaire is crucial for private placement offerings. Each type of offering has its own requirements for investors. An offering company must have a reasonable belief that the potential investors meet those requirements. That determination must be made before the potential investor can be given offering documents or specifics regarding the offering. This is done by having potential investors complete an investor questionnaire. The SEC has made it clear that a minimal "check the box" approach is not sufficient. In other words, you cannot have an investor questionnaire that merely asks "Are you an accredited investor?"

- The Subscription Agreement explains the terms and conditions of the offering. It is the "investment contract" for purchasing the securities. An investor will complete this document with Investor Questionnaire before writing a check.

- In debt offerings you need to have a Promissory Not outlining the terms of the loan arrangement with the investors. The note is the loan contract between the company and the investor.

3) Execute Filings

A Form D is filed with the SEC in Washington, DC. It notifies the SEC that you are using the Regulation D program and provides them basic information on the company and the offering. This is not a document seeking approval or registration; rather it is a filing that notifies the SEC that you have a Regulation D offering in the works; it is not difficult or expensive to prepare and file.

- Also called "Blue Sky" filings, most states require a specific form to be filed along with a copy of the SEC Form D and the PPM. States charge a small fee as well. The form does not need to be filed until capital has been received from an investor in that state, and typically just within 15 days of that date.

Marketing

The Reg D offering is now ready to market to investors. Special documentation is necessary for presenting to FINRA Broker/Dealers.

Regulation D is a series of six rules, Rules 501-506, establishing three transactional (that is, for the transaction, not for the company itself) exemptions from the registration requirements of the Securities Act of 1933.

Rule 504 applies to transactions in which up to $1 million of securities are sold in any twelve-month period. Rule 504 imposes no ceiling on the number of investors, permits the payment of commissions, and imposes no restrictions on the manner of offering or resale of securities. Further, Rule 504 does not prescribe specific disclosure requirements.

Generally, the intent of Rule 504 is to shift the obligation of regulating very small offerings to state "Blue Sky" administrators, though the offerings continue to be subject to Federal anti-fraud and civil liability provisions.

Rule 505 provides an exemption for offers and sales of securities totaling up to $5 million in any 12-month period. Under this exemption, securities may be sold to an unlimited number of "accredited investors" and up to 35 "unaccredited investors" who do not need to satisfy the sophistication or wealth standards associated with the other exemptions.

Purchasers must buy for investment only, not for resale. The securities are restricted in sense that investors may not sell them for at least two years. General solicitation or advertising to sell the securities is not allowed.

Rule 506 is available to all issuers for offerings sold to not more than thirty-five non-accredited purchasers and an unlimited number of accredited investors. Rule 506, however, unlike 504 and 505, requires an issuer to make subjective determinations.

CHAPTER SIX: S Corporation or C Corporation or Limited Liability Corporation?

Two of the most common legal business structures are the limited liability corporation (LLC) and the S corporation. There is also the C corporation. Your business will usually find that LLC offers advantages over both, at least at the outset.

Flexibility

An LLC allows a business to set up an ownership structure that makes sense for both business and tax purposes. Unlike an S Corp in which the share structure follows the amount invested by each shareholder, an LLC has more flexibility. This is important as profits flow through an LLC and are taxed in the hands of the owners. *Profit distribution does not need to mirror percentage investment in the company.*

Transfer of Ownership

In an S corporation, shares can be sold, gifted or willed to others, creating changes in ownership structure that can alter the direction of operations. An LLC is dissolved upon the bankruptcy or death of an owner; the other owners can then set up a new LLC.

Less Paperwork

Corporations, including S corps, are required to hold regular shareholder meetings and take minutes. A mandated board of directors make decisions via formal documented resolutions. An LLC operates under no requirement for minutes, resolutions or even board meetings. This gives the owner/manager more flexibility to make timely decisions. It also significantly reduces the time spent on administration chores as opposed to strategic planning and just doing business.

Lower State Filing Taxes

Although LLCs pay no federal income tax, state filing taxes are due. In almost all states, the annual state filing tax is less for LLCs than it is for S corps. In some states, LLCs with only two members do not pay any state filing tax. The minimum filing tax is always lower than it is for S corps.

Simple to Set Up

Forming an LLC is easy. The fees for setting it up are generally low. You gain the limited liability that you need and you get pass-through tax treatment without the "double taxation" of a C -Corp. Now you see why so many businesses start out as LLCs. However, as they grow, they usually change to C-Corporations; we will see why below.

S Corporation

The S Corporation is a popular structure for small businesses because the company is taxed like a sole proprietor or partnership. The company itself does not file its own taxes; instead, all company profits and losses are "passed through" and reported on the personal income tax return of the shareholders (or in the case of an LLC, the members).

While circumstances vary for each individual and his or her business, the following are general guidelines to help you;

1. Business Formality

With its roots as a C Corporation, the S Corporation involves formalities and compliance obligations, which can be burdensome for the solo entrepreneur. If you incorporate as an S Corporation, you need to set up a board of directors, file annual reports and other business filings, hold shareholder's meetings, keep records of your meetings' minutes and generally operates at a higher level of regulatory compliance than your business might need. LLCs use an informal operating agreement. If you want less red tape and formality, the LLC is for you, at least for now.

2. Who Can Be a Shareholder?

The S Corporation has more restrictions in terms of who can be a shareholder. For instance, S Corps cannot have more than 100 shareholders. Obviously, this is not relevant to most small businesses. In addition, all individual shareholders of an S Corp must be either U.S. citizens or permanent residents. If you have foreign owners or would like an LLC to be a shareholder you cannot form an S Corporation and probably should opt for the LLC.

3. Income Allocation

In an LLC, income and loss can be allocated disproportionately among the owners whereas in an S Corp income and loss are assigned to each shareholder based on their pro-rata shares of ownership.

This can be important. Say Joe and Jane open a software business as 50-50 owners. Time flies and Joe needs to focus on other things while Jane does almost all the all the work. Their business becomes profitable and it is time to divide up the profits. They decide Jane should keep 75% of the profits. With an LLC, everything is good, and Joe and Jane will be taxed pursuant to the terms of their LLC Operating Agreement.

But this will not work with an S Corporation. Since Joe and Jane are 50% owners, each will be allocated 50% of the corporation's income when it comes to computing income tax. If you need flexibility when it comes allocating profits among owners, the LLC is the structure for you.

4. Pass-Through Losses

With LLCs and S Corporations, members and shareholders pass company losses to their personal income. *Note that an LLC lets you pass more loss than does an S Corporation, most notably when it comes to real estate.* In an LLC used for real estate investments, members are allowed to add the amount of the mortgage to their basis for the purpose of computing a loss. If the business is real estate investments, the LLC permits writing off more losses on the personal tax returns.

5. Class of Stock

In an S Corporation, all shareholders own one class of stock. An S Corporation can have voting and non-voting shares but cannot have distinctions such as common stock and preferred stock. In an LLC, however, these priorities and preferences are allowed, and you can have different membership classes. You cannot offer common and preferred stock classes in an S Corporation. Again, if you want flexibility in ownership classification, you need an LLC.

6. Reinvesting Profits

As pass-through entities, individual owners of an S Corporation or an LLC are liable for any taxes owed on profits — whether that money is retained in the company or put in their wallets. For example, if you own 50% of an S Corporation and that company makes $100,000 in profit, you need to report $50,000 in income on your personal tax return. It does not matter whether that $50,000 actually ended up in your bank account. This is known as "phantom income" and can obviously cause problems on occasion.

If you plan on keeping money in the company and would prefer not to have be personally taxed on this money as a shareholder, you should consider the C Corporation over both the LLC and S Corp.

7. VC Funding

If your company is considering raising venture capital down the road, VC firms will most likely demand a C Corporation. Your business does not need to start as a

C Corp, but if: a) you are considering raising venture capital, and b) you start out with an LLC or an S Corp you will need to convert the business to a C Corp at some point. This conversion will require additional filings and fees within your state. If you choose this route, you may want to consider the S Corp as your initial option, since converting an S Corp to a C Corp can be done in a day with a single tax form.

Remember that tax treatment varies between states. Consulting with an accountant or CPA can help you determine which business structure offers the biggest advantages. Get your legal structure and planning straightened out as early as possible.

LLC vs. C-Corporation

The most obvious problem with C Corporations is that they do not offer the pass-through accounting that LLCs and S Corporations do, so the corporation will pay tax on any profits and employees and you will pay taxes on your salaries, and if there are any profit distributions by means of dividends you will be taxed again!

The tax code is not friendly to a C-Corporation that wants to provide profits to the shareholders in that if those shareholders are also employees, there will three different points of taxation, as we just saw.

LLCs look like they have only one point of taxation but in reality there is a second point of taxation because there is self-employment tax in addition to income tax. Of course paying self-employment tax is still better than paying a C-Corp tax because the C-Corp will need to make an employment tax on salaries which is essentially the same as the self-employment tax.

One difference is that with the C-Corp you can hold profits in the corporation rather than pay them out; therefore if you are highly profitable, you will want to hold profits in the corporation and also pay yourself a minimal salary. If you expect to experience losses as things ramp up, as it usually the case, the LLC has advantages. LLCs pass those losses along, and those loses can offset other income. In a C-corporation, the corporation will carry those losses (for credit against future profits) but the owner, as an tax-paying employee, does not get to make use of those losses. He or she will have W-2 income and will be taxed accordingly, just as if they were an employee anywhere else.

Still, the biggest limitation of LLCs is the systemic problem of how you deal with the ownership structure. LLCs do not have shareholders and shares of stock (instead they have "members" and "units"). It may seem that these are just different names for the same thing, but that is not so. In an LLC, one member is the same as another member. Everyone is working under the same operating agreement. An investor, the owner, other employees who have been given ownership -- all hold exactly the same share of equity or unit; there is no difference between them.

C - Corporations can issue different classes of stock, so an investor might have preferred stock and employees and owners have common stock. Those classes can be subdivided further so a investor today might get "Series A Preferred Stock" with certain rights and privileges, and later investors get "Series B Preferred Stock" with different rights. You might setup a stock option plan for employees to give them ownership in exchange for their work and loyalty to the company while the owners have founders stock. Vendors might get stock warrants in exchange for providing discounted services. In short, there is a lot more flexibility.

Then there are tax implications. If you have asked an investor to put in money at $10 per unit and later you give 100 units to an employee because you want to give them ownership, then you have subjected that employee to a tax hit. The IRS will say that you "gave" the employee $1000 worth of equity ($10 x 100 units) and he owes income tax--at ordinary income rates. So your employee is out, say, $300 + in taxes.

With the C-Corp, however, you can create a stock option plan to give ownership to employees. As long as the option price is equal to the fair market value of the underlying class of stock (at the time the option was granted) there is no taxable event. The expectation is that the company will grow, and by the time the stock vests it will be worth a lot more than when it was granted. The employee will have to pay tax on the gain if and when he/she exercises those options, but she/he does not need to exercise the options until they intend to cash in (and then there is cash to pay the tax!).

And it is taxed as capital gain (albeit short term), not as ordinary income. Note that in a C-Corporation all classes of stock are usually not created equal and, therefore, are not priced the same. If an investor buys preferred shares at $10/share that does not mean your common shares are also worth $10/share or that your base option price is $10/share. The preferred shares can have may benefits that make them much more valuable. Nobody would pay $10 for common when the same $10 can get them so much more with preferred.

Your board of directors will have set the price of common, as noted in the minutes, with an explanation of why they are worth so much less than the preferred shares. It is not unusual for this discount to be 90% (or more) in a start-up, so a $10 preferred price might mean $1 (or less) for common shares and their option exercise price!

So what do I do?

When Private Placement Advisors helps form a new company we start with an LLC. After success have been achieved and the entrepreneur wants to grant stock options to new (or old) employees or outside investors, we convert to a C-Corporation. When you are talking to major investors and employee option pools-Corporations are often the way to go. When it is only you and one or two partners at the outset, an LLC is what you want. But be careful with that LLC. You do not want to end up with a large number of investors who have invested at different times -- with no flexibility in how those shares/units are priced or structured.

CHAPTER SEVEN: Partnerships

The evolution of startup enterprises is generally: a) first, a partnership; b) second, an LLC; and c) finally a C Corporation or S Corporation. There are two types of partnerships: general and limited.

General Partnership

A partnership is a business relationship between at least two or more persons to carry on a business or a project. Each partner contributes money, property or skills and in exchange receives a share of the partnership's profits and losses. The partnership agreement specifies how the partnership will operate, the purpose of the partnership, how decisions will be made, and when distributions will be made. ·

Each partner has an equal right to participate in the management and control of the business. The partnership files an informational only annual income tax return. All profits and losses of the business pass to the personal income tax returns of the partners. Partners are not considered employees of the partnership.

Partnerships are easy to form and do not require formal document filings as do a corporation or a limited liability company. Partners are held personally, jointly and severally liable for all debts of the partnership, regardless of the percentage of ownership in the business. ·Upon the death, withdrawal, disability or resignation of any partner, the partnership by default will terminate.

All money or property contributed to the partnership becomes an asset of the partnership. All profits are shared with each partner.

Limited Partnership

The general partners deal with the day-to-day management of the business, and do not need to consult with or involve the limited partners for most business decisions. The profits and losses flow through the business to the partners, and pass to the personal income tax return of each partner.

A limited partner's liability for the debts of the partnership is limited to the amount of money or property she or he contributed to the partnership. Limited partners can leave or be replaced without the partnership being dissolved. General partners are held personally, jointly and severally liable for the business debts of the partnership. Limited partners are not responsible or liable for the general partners' misconduct or negligence.

Limited partners have liability protection from debts of the business similar to that of shareholders in a corporation. Each partner is responsible only for the amount of money he/she has contributed to the partnership. Like an LLC, a partnership files an informational only annual income tax return, and all profits and losses of the business will pass to the personal income tax returns of the partners. Some states restrict the types of professions that may form a limited partnership.

A limited partnership differs from a general partnership in that the partners do not share equal responsibility or liability for the business. This may be the ideal business model if you have investors who only wish to provide capital but not assume the responsibility of running a business.

Limited partners usually provide money and nothing else. This person will not have any say in how the business is run, but he/she will not have responsibility should something go wrong. In the case of more than one general partner, they will share the responsibilities. In a certificate of limited partnership, the general partners are named, while the limited partners are often kept anonymous. A certificate of limited partnership should include the following information:

- The name of the partnership must include the words "limited partnership" [cannot use the name of a limited partner]

- Address of the company office

- Name, address and written permission from the agent for service of process

- Name and business address of each general partner

- The date when the limited partnership will dissolve

- This document can open doors for business bank accounts and other business related activities.

CHAPTER EIGHT: Summary

"New Rules"

- Start-up companies now have new avenues for raising capital and investors will have more investment opportunities.

- General solicitation materials and publically advertised private placements must comply with new rules as well as with existing federal and state regulations.

- Some issuers will choose to rely on the "Old Rule 506" to raise capital.

- Private fund managers now have greater flexibility in marketing their funds.

Exhibit A: Engagement Letter (Immigration law firm and Private Placement Advisors)

Private Placement Advisors
5515 St. Helena Road
St. Helena, CA 95404
415.299.3277
www.privateplacementadvisors.com

—

[DATE]

Reference: ENGAGEMENT LETTER

[NAME], Esq.
The law Office of [NAME]
ADDRESS

Dear [Law Firm Name]:

The Law Office of -------------------------
------------ (the "Law Firm"] wishes to engage Private Placement Advisors ("PPA") to review, edit, and re-write as appropriate and practicable a private placement memorandum, investor questionnaire, as presently drafted and other offering documents yet to be drafted, prepared by the Law Firm on behalf

of   --------------------------------------
("the Client").

PPA understands that the subject offering documents are being prepared for a Regulation S, EB-5 Visa offering for the Client.

PPA has volunteered to the Law Firm that the following language is advisable if the Client is to have an online presence: "Access to this website is restricted to persons who are not U.S. citizens and who are located outside of the U.S., pursuant to Regulation S under the U.S. Securities Act of 1933, as amended (the "Securities Act"). Each person accessing this web site will be deemed to have understood and agreed that: (1) he or she is not a U.S. citizen and she or he is located outside of the U.S; (2) any securities described herein have not been and will not be registered under the Securities Act or with any securities regulatory authority of any state, and may not be transferred to any U.S. citizen unless the securities are registered under the Securities Act, or an exemption from the registration requirements of the Securities Act are available."

Douglas Slain, a retired member of the California Bar, has qualifications that include: a) publisher/editor of *Securities Enforcement Reporter* and *Blue Sky Chronicle*; b) owner/manager of the 1300 member "Securities Enforcement and Regulation LinkedIn Discussion Group"; c) manager of regDconsumersreport.com, a blog that explores and questions the new SEC Rule 506(c) among other topics; and, d) author of a numerous handbooks for lawyers and other professionals, including *EB-5 and U.S. Securities Law; Real Estate Blind Pools,* and *Exempt Offerings for Feature Films.* Slain has been asked to serve as an expert witness in litigation involving SEC Rule 506(b). Other contractors and associates with whom PPA associates with on a project-by-project basis may or may not be certified public accountants or licensed securities professionals.

This confirms that Law Firm agrees to pay PPA $125/hour for editorial and consulting services with a $1,000 retainer.

Cordially,

Private Placement Advisors

By: _____

Douglas Slain

Managing Partner

Exhibit B: Opinion Letter to Confirm Accredited Investor Verification

Private Placement Advisors

5515 St. Helena Rd

St. Helena, CA 95404

415.299.3277

www.regDconsumersreport.com /

www.privateplacementadvisors.com

[Date]

[Client name and address]

Reference: Opinion Letter for Accredited Investor Verification

Dear Sir/Madame:

[Client name] ("Client") has asked Private Placement Advisors ("PPA") for an opinion letter based on the facts set forth below to help determine whether or not Client has taken reasonable steps to confirm that [name of investor] ("Investor") is an accredited investor as defined in Rule 501(a) under the Securities Act of 1933.

Client understands that the SEC has not yet offered either a uniform verification method or a non-comprehensive list of verification methods to satisfy its verification requirement. Client acknowledges that a determination of whether verification steps taken in a given transaction were "reasonable" is based in significant part on particular facts and circumstances surrounding each transaction. Client understands that the determination of whether a person is an accredited investor is a factual question to which a legal opinion does not obtain nor apply.

Client understands that in addition to the minimum income and net worth requirements, the Client needs to consider the type of Investor and the amount and type of information that the Client has about the Investor. Client understands that the more information that it has indicating that an Investor is accredited, the fewer steps will be necessary to verify an Investor's eligibility.

Client understands that the methods through which an issuer has publicly solicited investors through Rule 506(c) general advertising may be relevant in determining the reasonableness of the steps it takes to verify the accredited investor status of investors. (For instance, an issuer that solicits new investors through a website accessible to the general public, or through social media solicitation, will be required to undertake more stringent verification steps than an issuer that solicits investors from a database of "screened" accredited investors aintained by a "reasonably reliable" third-party).

Client further understands that the terms of an offering may be relevant. (For example, setting a high minimum investment amount requirement per investor, especially with a direct cash investment that is not financed, so that only accredited investors could reasonably be expected to risk losing their entire investment, further verifies accredited investor status).

Client further understands that the Client bears the burden of establishing the availability of an SEC Regulation D exemption. PPA does not make any representation about whether this letter is sufficient for Client's purposes.

This confirms that Client has reviewed the original or copies of the following documents:

1. Joint tax returns for the years 2011 and 2012 (each, a "Tax Year") filed by Client and [his/her] spouse on Form 1040 (the "Tax Returns"), accompanied by a certificate signed by the Client, attached hereto and addressed to us, attesting that the copies of the Tax Returns provided are true, correct and complete, filed with the appropriate office of the Internal Revenue Service, prepared in full compliance with applicable law and governmental regulations and have not been amended.

2. A certificate executed by Client and [his/her] spouse, attached hereto, and addressed to us, stating such persons have a

reasonable expectation of joint income in the current year in excess of $300,000.

PPA has not conducted any other investigation or inquiries of Client, and has not determined whether the Tax Returns were accurately prepared, or agree with source documents, or were properly filed. This letter is limited to the matters set forth herein and speaks only as of the date hereof. Nothing may be inferred or implied beyond the matters expressly contained herein. This confirms [fact pattern that applies to steps taken to determine accredited investor status].

Based on the totality of the information provided, it is the opinion of PPA that Client has taken reasonable steps to establish that Investor is an accredited investor under SEC Regulation D. The managing partner of Private Placement Advisors is qualified to provide this opinion based on the professional qualifications attached to this opinion letter and as cited at www.privateplacementadvisors.com under "About Us."

This letter may be relied upon by Client only in connection with an offering under Rule 506(c) and only for 30 days from the date of this letter. This letter may not be used, quoted from, referred to or relied upon by you or by any other person for any other purpose, nor may copies be delivered to any other person, without in each instance express prior written consent of PPA. We assume no obligation to update this letter.

Cordially,

Private Placement Advisors

By: _____

Douglas Slain

Managing Partner

About the author

After getting a JD from Stanford Law School, a MA from the University of Chicago, a diploma from the University College London, and working as a reporter for The Wall Street Journal, Doug was a member of the California bar for 40 years, during which time he founded a series of law reporting services now owned by Thomson-Reuters. Doug specializes in debt and equity crowdfunding. He helps small business identify and solicit sources of private equity. Doug monitors a LinkedIn discussion group, State Securities Regulation, with 1500 members.

Connect with Douglas Slain:

LinkedIn: http://linkedin.com/in/douglasslain
Facebook: http://facebook.com/douglas.slain
Twitter: https://twitter.com/exemptofferings
Blog: http://www.privateplacementadvisors.com/apps/blog
Web site: http://privateplacementadvisors.com

www.ingramcontent.com/pod-product-compliance
Lightning Source LLC
Chambersburg PA
CBHW071637170526
45166CB00003B/1350